FORGIVENESS

Picking Up the Pieces

Grace

WestBow
PRESS
A DIVISION OF THOMAS NELSON

Scripture quotations taken from the Holy Bible, New Living Translation, copyright 1996, 2004. Used by permission of Tyndale House Publishers, Inc., Wheaton, Illinois 60189. All rights reserved.

Scripture taken from the Amplified Bible, Copyright © 1954, 1958, 1962, 1964, 1965, 1987 by The Lockman Foundation. Used by permission.

The Ryrie Study Bible King James Version 1976, 1978 by The Moody Bible Institute of Chicago

WestBow Press books may be ordered through booksellers or by contacting:

WestBow Press
A Division of Thomas Nelson
1663 Liberty Drive
Bloomington, IN 47403
www.westbowpress.com
1-(866) 928-1240

Because of the dynamic nature of the Internet, any web addresses or links contained in this book may have changed since publication and may no longer be valid. The views expressed in this work are solely those of the author and do not necessarily reflect the views of the publisher, and the publisher hereby disclaims any responsibility for them.

Any people depicted in stock imagery provided by Thinkstock are models, and such images are being used for illustrative purposes only.

Certain stock imagery © Thinkstock.

ISBN: 978-1-4497-6291-9 (sc)
ISBN: 978-1-4497-6292-6 (e)

Library of Congress Control Number: 2012914701

Printed in the United States of America

WestBow Press rev. date: 08/22/2012

One of the Pharisees asked Jesus to have dinner with him, so Jesus went to his home and sat down to eat. When a certain immoral woman from that city heard he was eating there, she brought a beautiful alabaster jar filled with expensive perfume. Then she knelt behind him at his feet, weeping. Her tears fell on his feet, and she wiped them off with her hair. Then she kept kissing his feet and putting perfume on them. When the Pharisee who had invited him saw this, he said to himself, "If this man were a prophet, he would know what kind of woman is touching him. She's a sinner!" Then Jesus answered his thoughts. "Simon," he said to the Pharisee, "I have something to say to you." "Go ahead. Teacher," Simon replied. Then Jesus told him this story: "A man loaned money to two people-500 pieces of silver to one and 50 pieces to the other. But neither of them could repay him, so he kindly forgave them both, canceling their debts. Who do you suppose loved him more after that?" Simon answered, "I suppose the one for whom he canceled the larger debt."

"That's right," Jesus said. Then he turned to the woman and said to Simon, "Look at this woman kneeling here. When I entered your home, you didn't offer me water to wash the dust from my feet, but she has washed them with her tears and wiped them with her hair. You didn't greet me with a kiss, but from the time I first came in, she has not stopped kissing my feet. You neglected the courtesy of olive oil to anoint my head, but she has anointed my feet with rare perfume. I tell you her sins-and they are many- have been forgiven, so she has shown me much love. But a person who is forgiven little shows only little love. Then Jesus said to the woman, "Your sins are forgiven."

Luke 7: 36-50

Contents

Overcoming Guilt, Rage, and Depression
My Personal Story

The first emotion I ever remember feeling was pride. I was proud of myself because I could smoke cigarettes, do drugs, and drink alcohol like everybody else. I found that when I used drugs I could numb feelings and memories and I had friends. I also remember losing my innocence at age four. I wanted to forget that memory. Also, I wanted to find friends. Friends were the most important thing in my life when I was growing up because I had lived a life of isolation during my teenage years.

Maybe there are other reasons you have turned to idols. Everybody does. We all stray. Maybe you suffer from guilt. Maybe you have or have had violence in your home. Maybe you are a soldier with survivor's guilt. My idols were sex, drugs, and rock-n-roll. It almost killed me in the end. At first, my motivation was to have friends and be accepted by other people so I would not be so lonely. Then I began to try to escape reality and, in the end, it was revenge. I was out to conquer and hurt every man on the planet because I felt like a victim. As the years went by, the more revenge and anger I felt on the inside, the more horrific my life became on the outside. The more horrific my life became on the outside, the more revenge and anger I felt on the inside. It was a vicious cycle.

In 1978 I was kidnapped by organized crime. I was beaten, starved, held hostage, screamed at, forced into pornography, and threatened with death daily. The daily dose of fear was horrific. Everything my husband and I owned, and all the money we had in the bank, was stolen. And I was brainwashed into believing I was going to be a "rock star". For about one year I was stalked (1977-78) and then for one year (1978-79), I was held hostage. When nothing was left for them to take I sold my soul and joined their family and in return, they allowed me to live. In 1979 I came home. I was destroyed. I was divorced for the second time by age 21 with unbearable guilt and shame. I was penniless, and my mind had snapped. I did not even have my own soul.

In 1979, after I came home, I went to a church that was having a lot of miracles happening in the congregation. It was called the "Spirit of Love Church." I got my soul and salvation back according to James 5:19, 20.

My dear brothers and sisters, if someone among you wanders away from the truth and is brought back, you can be sure that whoever brings the sinner back will save that person from death and bring about the forgiveness of many sins. James 5:19-20

If you have ever committed that sin, selling your soul or denying Christ, I am inviting you back to wholeness so that you may serve Christ and go to heaven, justified, and as righteous as Christ Himself with forgiveness of all your sins.

That was a beginning and I was so happy. I even went to Discipleship and Missionary School at Agapeforce for one year. Yet, when I left, I had to face the drugs, drink, and mental illness again and I was fighting a losing battle. I was also raped by a member of the "Spirit of Love" church and kicked out of Agapeforce's Missionary School, so I gave up and left the church.

In 1980, I found myself locked up in a mental hospital. The diagnosis was mental illness due to an overdose of cocaine. The doctors and therapists told me I had a chemical imbalance in my brain because I had done too many drugs. Then I was placed on medication and therapy for addiction to drugs and alcohol. During these deep dark days I lost everything and everyone except my immediate family. Then, for the next 32 years, God reached down from heaven; healing, blessing, teaching, and leading me on an adventure. Life has steadily gotten better and better even though for the first few years I saw no difference in my life.

In 1980, when I got locked up I lost all my friends along with most of my family's loyalty and friendship. I was "marked" and no one wanted anything to do with me. I found I could no longer do simple things like: find and hold a job, function without medication and therapy, lose weight, nor go back to school and finish. At first I thought everything was normal, didn't everybody drink, do drugs, and sleep around? That was normal life for me and I kept trying to find my answers in Education. When I found I could not stop the drugs and alcohol, or find and hold a job, or finish school, I was hopeless. Then, after I did sober up, ten years later, I felt it was everyone else's fault. I blamed everyone else and I had a hard time looking at myself. I could not look myself in the mirror, or look at what I was doing in daily life, without remorse and guilt for the things I was doing or had done. I felt I was a victim and I wanted revenge. Revenge, depression, anger, and hopelessness usually bring about violence against the one's we love then often times suicide or murder. This attitude brought me, terrible sexual perversions, but God was patient and merciful.

I tried one last time to marry and have a family in 1984. I thought living the "Christian Life" would be my salvation. At my son's birth in 1989, his Daddy and I were in divorce proceedings and it was my third divorce. The guilt I felt was unbearable. I called it quits on marriage and brought up my son with my immediate family's help, especially with my Mother's love and wisdom.

November 15, 1989 I took my last drink and sobered up. I had become suicidal and was using alcohol to cope. It was always a choice between suicide and alcohol until that Thursday night. I was trying with all my heart and soul to sober up and lead a "normal Christian life." But I could not do it. That night at 7:15 God met me in His mercy, anointed me for service, and gave me the peace that passes all understanding. He gave me His presence and love. That was my last drink. God began giving me the grace to forgive myself and others for the first time in my life and I began to experience peace like I had never known. Only God could rescue me and turn my life around. He came through for me. He will come through for you, too. He always comes through. We can trust Him. We just need to ask, seek, and knock. He has the answers we need in His Word, the Bible. And I am convinced that, in or out of church, we can find the forgiveness, sanity, blessings, and abundant life God promises no matter the struggle, no matter who is for or against us, God holds the victory.

Life is a journey and not all my problems were solved by being sober and clean. Even though I no longer used drugs and alcohol I still had to learn how to live. For example, I was a victim of violence in my own family from two veterans who were suffering from P.T.S.D and had to deal with rage on my part, too. But again, God came through. Forgiveness for my enemies, what Jesus taught, was the key to the violence at home. Prayer, self-preservation, and forgiveness were the keys. Sometimes it took separation and difficult choices, sometimes it took self-respect. I will talk more about this later. And I had no work ethics nor had I held a job in thirty years when I had to go out in the world and work. Also, I had no common sense because I had been dishonest and dependent all my life. But God came through. It does not matter the obstacle to overcome, Jesus is the answer. And my mind was restored when I needed it most. God is never late. He is always on time and meets every need: physical, emotional, mental, spiritual, financial, and in relationships.

I had been saved as a child and tried to live the "Christian Life" for many years but it took the Baptism of the Holy Spirit to give me the grace and power to overcome sin and bitterness. I do not believe I would have lived through some of the things I experienced without the power and protection of the Holy Ghost.

Today, I have 22 years without alcohol and illegal drugs. I have been celibate for 20 years and I have a job and I work. I graduated from College with honors in an A.A.S. Degree in Drug and Alcohol Counseling and I am licensed by the State of Texas as a Counselor Intern. I never remarried. This is the happiest time in my life. My son is in the army and has served one year in Iraq. My son wants to make the military his career. We buried my Mother in 2007 and I miss her, but I was not destroyed. God came through.

I come from a military family. My son's father served peace-time Marines for four years, my father served in WWII and Korea, retiring after 20 years in the Air Force. My brother served voluntarily in Vietnam and now my son is serving. I have experienced picking up the pieces after someone comes home and seen the damage it can do to a veteran and his family many times.

Love and forgiveness go together. You cannot have love without forgiveness and you cannot have forgiveness without love. There are very few Veterans who find recovery and hope after coming home without God's love, forgiveness, and hope. The Veteran needs mercy, guidance, love, hope and forgiveness for himself and those around him. Honor only goes so far. Our Veteran's need more courage to face life after coming home than they did when they deployed for the first time. The feeling in the airport is, "What do I do now?"

If I have hit a nerve......read this little book. I pray you see another side of life, one of hope, joy and peace.

Grace

"Impossible"

Many times while reading this book, you may say to yourself, "This is impossible, I can't live up to all this…" May I give you some comfort and encouragement? It is the grace of God, not our "works," that fulfill the plans and commands of God. We cannot keep the commands God requires of us, it is the power of God's Spirit that comes into our hearts and lives and fulfills the things required. We cannot live up to them. No will power or self-confidence can fulfill God's requirements. Only God's grace can bring about the miracles. We just do the footwork outlined in this book and then the Bible and God do the miracles. Keep an open mind, pray, keep reading, and use the tools and instructions in this book not just once but keep practicing love and forgiveness the rest of your life. Love and forgiveness are life-long journeys and without God's help, we keep making the same mistakes over and over. Keep an open mind and keep reading. Hopefully you will use this little book more than once.

Grace

Salvation and Baptism in the Holy Spirit
THIS BEGINS THE HEALING

First, I had to come to God and ask for his help. In prayer I turned my heart, will, and life over to Him and cried out for Him to heal me and make some sense out of my life. I asked for His mercy and grace. Then He gave me the Baptism of the Holy Spirit. I did not know what that was but I was desperate to try anything and so, out of simple child-like trust, I was baptized over the phone and I spoke in an unknown, heavenly prayer language. My Mother had called the "700 Club" for prayer. I was ready and willing, even though I had never even heard of the Baptism of the Holy Ghost. The counselor over the phone from the "700 Club" knew exactly what I needed and I trusted her. At the time, all I knew was I was about to face death and I was not ready. I believe because of my child-like faith and acceptance of the Baptism of the Holy Spirit, God gave me a second chance and I found power in my walk with God. I now look at my past life and see that without God's power I would never have been able to escape death or recover and learn my basic flaw of not being able to love and forgive. I had to be desperate enough to realize that God was the only hope I had. He was the only one who could save me from myself. I had to admit I needed help and was determined to do whatever was necessary to change.

When I kept doing the same things over and over, I kept getting the same results over and over, yet worse every time. I kept digging holes deeper and deeper and then falling into them. Three divorces, mental illness, nicotine addiction, drug and alcohol addictions, sexual addictions, and other perversions were getting worse until I was staring death in the face and I was not ready to die. So, I cried out to God and I was willing to do whatever he told me to do. I was hopeless. God then began directing my life.

There was only one who I knew had the power to change me and get me out of the mess I was in and that was Jesus. He died to set us free from living hell. He came through for me. So, I suggest, that if you need a new life and a second chance, give your heart to Jesus and ask for the Holy Spirit's Baptism that only Jesus can give. This will give you power to change and overcome sin. This can give you a new life. This life is worth living.

If you have "tried church" and found no power but only guilt and loneliness-don't give up on God. His people are flawed and imperfect but Jesus is perfect. God and His ways are perfect, strong, powerful, all wise, merciful, just, righteous, fair, loving, tenderhearted, patient, and longsuffering. Jesus was <u>always</u> "hanging out with the sinners."

God loves you so much that he gave his one and only begotten Son to leave heaven and come down as an innocent child. Jesus grew up as a perfect man, never sinned, and then died a horrible, painful death as a sacrifice for you. He removed all curses that were brought into the world by satan and his kingdom. Jesus defeated satan, all his demonic realm, sin, death, and all hell itself. Then Jesus came back to life again and sent out his Word, the Bible, and his disciples to tell everyone of the Good News. Jesus had won the battle and made Blessings available to all who wanted a new life, here on earth, as well as eternal life in heaven with him.

Prayer for Salvation and Baptism of the Holy Spirit and Fire

"Jesus, come into my heart and life. Please make me a new creature, born again, and I make you my Lord. I ask your forgiveness for all my sin and please baptize me in the Holy Spirit and fire. Please grant me a heavenly language of prayer, tongues, so that I may praise and worship you in Spirit and in truth. Place a call on my life and grant me guidance and wisdom. May I have strong hope and give hope to all I touch, in word and deed. Grant me grace to overcome my trials on earth and please accept my soul after death. Open my eyes and heart to the needs all around me and as I unselfishly give to others, meet my needs and heart's desires. Grant me the abundant life that Jesus promised in John 10 and help me to obey your commands of love in your Word. Keep me humble and safe. Grant me the wisdom, grace, deliverance, and power to overcome all the enemies' temptations and deceptions, satan and all his demonic realm. May I live a life of victory and blessing as you promised in Deuteronomy 28: 1-14. Thank you for hearing and answering all of my prayers and heart's cry knowing what I need before even I do."

"In Jesus' precious, holy name and blood,"

Amen

Now write in today's date and a few notes to remember the beginning of this new and wonderful life.

_____

_____

_____

_____

_____

_____

_____

_____

A Root of Evil

I Timothy 6: 10 in the Amplified does NOT say, "For the love of money is THE root of ALL evil." NO, NO!! I Timothy 6: 10 in the Amplified Bible says, *"For the love of money is A root of all evils."* Not forgiving ourselves and others around us is another root of evil. Let's take a look at some of the evil it can cause:

1. Anger

2. Resentment

3. Depression

4. Broken relationships

5. Broken families

6. Murder

7. Mental illness

8. Self-hatred

9. Self-loathing

10. Distorted self-esteem

11. Alcoholism

12. Failure at work

13. Failure at home in the family

14. No peace of mind or heart

15. Bitterness

16. Violence

17. Sickness and disease

18. Broken hearts

19. Suicide

20. Crime

21. Self-pity

22. Pride

23. Distorted self-image

24. Drug addiction

25. Obesity

26. Poverty

27. Divorce

28. Goals and dreams destroyed

29. Hatred

30. Blame

31. Personal growth stopped

32. Unanswered prayers

33. Fear

Those are some of the more obvious problems. Some people have a difficult time in forgiving themselves and others and it destroys. That is why I wrote this little book to give you some simple tools for you to get started in forgiving yourself and others around you and so you may be free and forgetful of the hurt and pain that life has thrown your way. Whether you are a soldier returning from battle, or a Mother waiting patiently, these steps and tools can help you have better survival techniques in what you are about to face. It takes work to forgive but after practicing forgiveness for a while it then becomes as important as breathing air because of the peace in mind, spirit, soul, and body. Forgiveness produces joy and the fruit of the Spirit. Our prayers are answered more quickly and we do not seek revenge but allow God to protect and avenge the wrongs others have done. Spiritual gifts cannot flow until all sin and bitterness is surrendered at the cross. We have to empty our feelings out to a merciful and loving Father so He can give us the peace we seek and need in our daily lives. So what do we do first?

Forgiving Myself First

I needed to see my own faults and character defects. I also needed to learn how to forgive myself before I could have the tools to forgive others. First, I was hard on myself. I dwelt on my own faults first. I wrote them down. Then I found a trustworthy, listening ear so I could confess my own faults and allow someone to see my vulnerable side. This is the only way God could get in and change my character. His merciful grace and the Word of God, the Bible, command us to do this.

"Confess your sins to each other and pray for each other so that you may be healed. The earnest prayer of a righteous person has great power and produces wonderful results." James 5: 16

"If we claim we have no sin, we are only fooling ourselves and not living the truth. But if we confess our sins to him, he is faithful and just to forgive us our sins and to cleanse us from all wickedness." I John I: 8, 9

Soon, it will be time to write down my faults, mistakes, character defects and sins on a piece of paper then find someone who can keep a confidence to share my secrets without holding anything back. After I practiced this for some time, I found honesty was priceless. Proverbs promises that with honesty we develop common sense. As I practiced humility (not humiliation-another word for humility is honesty), wisdom was my reward.

One tool that has helped me through the years is in keeping a journal. Many successful people keep a journal. I started with a journal to help me see how some of my thought patterns produced unwarranted fear and I was able to replace those thoughts with kind words toward myself and find comfort and trust in my own thoughts. All of my harmful thinking can be replaced with the goodness of God. My journal in later years has become my prayer journal and I use it to talk to God. The Apostle Paul's journals were his letters to the Christians around the world.

"And now, dear brothers and sisters, one final thing. Fix your thoughts on what is true, and honorable, and right, and pure, and lovely, and admirable. Think about things that are excellent and worthy of praise.

Keep putting into practice all you learned and received from me-everything you heard from me and saw me doing. Then the God of peace will be with you." Philippians 4: 8, 9

The rewards are God's presence, peace, common sense, and wisdom.

After we have learned to forgive ourselves then we can move on and learn how to forgive others. We can only have understanding, mercy, compassion, humility, forgiveness, honesty, and truth towards others after we have stopped beating up on ourselves.

Jesus replied, "You must love the Lord your God with all your heart, all your soul, and all your mind. This is the first and greatest commandment. A second is equally important. Love your neighbor as yourself." Matthew 22: 37-39

We can only love others as much as we honestly love ourselves. We have to practice forgiving ourselves until we see ourselves as good. We need to be satisfied with progress, not perfection, because love and forgiveness are life-long lessons. It is in the journey that we find our destination. We have to know ourselves before we can come to know our Creator intimately. Remember the Prodigal Son. Remember, too, all things work together for the good for those called according to his purpose.

To illustrate the point further, Jesus told them this story. "A man had two sons. The younger son told his father, 'I want my share of your estate now before you die.' So his father agreed to divide his wealth between his sons. A few days later this younger son packed all his belongings and moved to a distant land, and there he wasted all his money in wild living. About the time his money ran out, a great famine swept over the land. And he began to starve. He persuaded a local farmer to hire him, and the man sent him into his fields to feed the pigs. The young man became so hungry that even the pods he was feeding the pigs looked good to him. But no one gave him anything. When he finally came to his senses he said to himself. 'At home even the hired servants have food enough to spare, and here I am dying of hunger. I will go home to my father and say, "Father I have sinned against both heaven and you, and I am no longer worthy of being called your son. Please take me on as a hired servant."'

"So he returned home to his father. And while he was still a long way off, his father saw him coming. Filled with love and compassion, he ran to his son, embraced him, and kissed him. His son said to him, 'Father, I have sinned against both heaven and you, and I am no longer worthy of being called your son. '

"But his father said to the servants, 'Quick! Bring the finest robe in the house and put it on him. Get a ring for his finger and sandals for his feet. And kill the calf we have been fattening. We must celebrate with a feast, for this son of mine was dead and has now returned to life. He was lost, but now he is found. So the party began."

Luke 15: 11- 24 Jesus.

Love and Forgiveness

Growing in love and forgiveness is a life-long process. When I first began writing my emotions and faults and mistakes and sins down on a piece of paper it flowed like a personal story. That is good. At first, I just wrote everything that haunted me. I soon found I was angry with myself most of all. I was like the Apostle Paul who viewed himself as the "chief of all sinners" and the most unworthy.

Then, in later years, I began 'blaming' everyone else. It was all, 'their fault.' I was a victim! Someone, much wiser than I, showed me how I was a "volunteer" and not a "victim". I had placed myself in a position to be hurt or just took offense at what someone else did or said. Also, I was not looking at the situation from the other person's point of view. I had to be 'right' all the time. I was always 'talking' and never 'listening.' I was what the Bible calls a 'fool', and an 'immoral woman'.

But, I could not blame someone else for my life's decisions, my emotions, for my attitude, words and actions. As it has been said before, "You made up your own bed and now you have to lie in it." It was my own thoughts, words, actions, and decisions that caused me all the grief and heartache in my life. Jesus said it this way,

"A good person produces good things from the treasury of a good heart, and an evil person produces evil things from the treasury of an evil heart." Matthew 12: 35

"Don't you understand yet?" Jesus asked. "Anything you eat passes through the stomach and then goes into the sewer. But the words you speak come from the heart-that's what defile you. For from the heart come evil thoughts, murder, adultery, all sexual immorality, theft, lying, and slander. These are what defile you. Eating with unwashed hands will never defile you." Matthew 15: 16-20 Jesus.

It is what is in our hearts that decide our destiny because what is in our hearts comes out our mouths and shapes our destiny. Listen to what you are saying. Listen to your heart. Jesus taught that our words coming from our hearts defile us. Our hearts need cleansing and holiness. Our hearts are our secret thoughts. What we dwell on and think about determines our attitude, thoughts, words, and deeds. That is where sin is born, in our hearts. Our attitude and secret thoughts give birth to sin and it comes out of our mouths, and affects everything. Our actions and decisions are based on our thoughts and words. That is why we are commanded to think on the pure and lovely by the Apostle Paul. It is spiritual law.

"And now, dear brothers and sisters, one final thing. Fix your thoughts on what is true, and honorable, and right, and pure, and lovely, and admirable. Think about things that are excellent and worthy of praise." Philippians 4: 8

This is how we grow holy. To love and forgive so we can honestly think and say good things from our heart. Then, our thoughts, desires, words, attitudes, actions, and decisions change and become holy before the Lord. This is a life worth living. It affects everything.

Christ died on the cross and sent the Holy Spirit to give us the power to change and since satan is defeated we have the ability to overcome <u>all</u> evil. He, Jesus, not only died for our sins to be forgiven because of God's love for us, but also for us to have the power to change and become righteous, good, and holy in His sight. He wants us to have a wonderful life on earth <u>in this life</u> <u>time</u>. Jesus and the Father desire that we become holy and follow Jesus' example of living on this earth during our life time. He gives an abundant life full of joy and thanksgiving because he is a good God. He is loving and kind and tenderhearted. He gave us the Holy Spirit so we could have the power to live out the example Christ gave us, changing and not making the same mistakes and sins over and over again. We are supposed to be going from "glory to glory," changing and growing becoming more and more like Christ. If we are not growing and becoming more like Jesus, then something is wrong. Maybe we need to look in our hearts and make sure there is no bitterness. It takes love and forgiveness ruling in our hearts and minds so that we can understand and love Jesus and others more and more fully. When we begin to love Jesus with our hearts we can then begin loving ourselves. Once we begin loving ourselves, then we learn how to love others.

We are not just forgiven to do whatever we want but we are responsible for obeying the commands Jesus gave us and one of them was *"...be ye perfect, as your heavenly Father is perfect."* Jesus was talking about loving your enemies and being good to them. This cannot be done unless there is love and forgiveness in our hearts for them. It will be reflected in our hearts, words, actions, and attitude. Love and forgiveness are inseparable. <u>There can be no forgiveness without love and there can be no love without forgiveness.</u>

Forgiveness Commanded

The blessings in Deuteronomy 28 are conditional that we fulfill the commandments of God. If we do not obey the commands then there are curses listed. There is great reward in obedience to God. We are given those commandments in the New Testament.

"'You must love the Lord your God with all your heart, all your soul, and all your mind.' This is the first and greatest commandment. A second is equally important. 'Love your neighbor as yourself.' The entire law and all the demands of the prophets are based on these two commandments." Matthew 22: 37-40

We are to love our enemies. We can still be warriors and soldiers and serve God. Many nations, 32 Kings and their kingdoms, were wiped off the face of the earth by God and Israel in war to possess their promised land. And do not forget Moses and the Egyptians. There is a time to fight and there is a time to come home. A soldier obeys God and protects his country, family, and friends just like a policeman. A murderer kills and destroys because of rage, anger, self-centeredness, and selfish, hateful reasons. We can pray for our enemies and yet still fight and kill them in obedience to God and our country. God made war. It was His idea in the first place. He has a reason for war and death. There is nothing wrong in protecting your loved ones. To forgive, after coming home, is important. Just do not kill for the sake of killing. Do not kill the innocent. Do not hurt others when they have done you no wrong, especially after coming home. And if you have hurt, or killed an innocent person, there is forgiveness for you. Get with your leaders who are Christians, find out how they pray for their enemies, yet fight. King David started out as a shepherd boy. In his first battle, he killed a giant in war, and gave the Israelites victory over the Philistines. He won King Saul's favor, and King Saul later betrayed David and chased him for years trying to kill him. King David killed thousands of men, yet God Himself, called David "a man after God's own heart." God and David were so close, and David had so much favor in God's eyes, that God promised King David that the Messiah would be one of his own descendants. David was tested time after time, while King Saul was trying to kill him. But

David proved loyal and would not touch King Saul. King Saul was anointed to be King, so David prayed for him and refused to hurt him. King David was loyal to God and yet, probably killed over 10,000 men in battle without even being wounded. King David, like us all, had his downfall. He committed sin by taking Bathsheba into his bed, then had her husband killed in battle to cover up a pregnancy. Their baby died and David paid a great price, in his family, for his sins.

"You have heard the law that says, 'Love your neighbor' and hate your enemy. But I say, love your enemies! Pray for those who persecute you! In that way, you will be acting as true children of your Father in heaven. For he gives his sunlight to both the evil and the good, and he sends rain on the just and the unjust alike. If you love only those who love you, what reward is there for that? Even corrupt tax collectors do that much. If you are kind to only your friends, how are you different from anyone else? Even pagans do that. But you are to be perfect even as your Father in heaven is perfect." Matthew 5:43-48 Jesus.

The Lord will not answer our prayers and faith does not work if we refuse to forgive from the heart. For example, we have heard many times sermons on 'speaking to the mountains' with our faith and prayers yet, I have never heard a sermon on Mark 11:25. Let's take a closer look at that scripture.

Then Jesus said to the disciples, "Have faith in God. I tell you the truth, you can say to this mountain, 'May you be lifted up and thrown into the sea', and it will happen. But you must really believe it will happen and have no doubt in your heart. I tell you, you can pray for anything, and if you believe that you've received it, it will be yours. BUT WHEN YOU ARE PRAYING, FIRST FORGIVE ANYONE YOU ARE HOLDING A GRUDGE AGAINST, SO THAT YOUR FATHER IN HEAVEN WILL FORGIVE YOUR SINS, TOO." Mark 11: 22-25 Jesus.

Our faith and prayers can be hindered by even a small grudge against someone, enemy or friend. The King James Version it is taken a step further and is made clear by verse 26.

"BUT IF YE DO NOT FORGIVE, NEITHER WILL YOUR FATHER WHICH IS IN HEAVEN FORGIVE YOUR TRESPASSES." Mark 11:26 King James Version. Jesus.

Yes, you can forgive your enemies and fight against them in battle, it is possible. And forgiveness is vital in having peace with ourselves and others. And the giving to God also depends on our forgiveness of ourselves and others. That means our tithes and finances can be hindered and not accepted. No wonder we do not have victory financially. Satan has had a death grip on our money and we did not know why. Now we know.

"So if you are presenting a sacrifice at the altar in the Temple and you suddenly remember that someone has something against you, leave your sacrifice there at the altar. Go and be reconciled to that person. Then come and offer your sacrifice to God." Matthew 5: 21- 26 Jesus.

Studying that scripture in context we notice that Jesus is talking about forgiveness. Also, Jesus gave us a teaching about forgiving in our finances. Jesus gave us this parable.

"Therefore, the Kingdom of Heaven can be compared to a king who decided to bring his accounts up to date with servants who had borrowed money from him. In the process, one of his debtors was brought in who owed him millions of dollars. He couldn't pay, so his master ordered that he be sold-along with his wife, his children, and everything he owned-to pay the debt. But the man fell down before his master and begged him, 'Please be patient with me, and I will pay it all.' Then his master was filled with pity for him and he released him and forgave his debt. But when the man left the king, he went to a fellow servant who owed him a few thousand dollars. He grabbed him by the throat and demanded instant payment. His fellow servant fell down before him and begged for a little more time. 'Be patient with me, and I will pay it.' He pleaded. But his creditor wouldn't wait. He had the man arrested and put in prison until the debt could be paid in full. When some of the other servants saw this, they were very upset. They went to the king and told him everything that had happened. Then the king called in the man he had forgiven and said, 'You evil servant! I forgave you that tremendous debt because you pleaded with me. Shouldn't you have mercy on your fellow servant, just as I had mercy on you?' Then the angry king sent the man to prison to be tortured until he had paid his entire debt. That's what my heavenly Father will do to you if you refuse to forgive your brothers and sisters from your heart." Matthew 18: 23-35 Jesus.

Not only does this scripture deal with money but also judgment and forgiveness. If we do not forgive those who have done us wrong financially then the Lord God will not forgive our debts. We cannot hold even a small grudge against anyone. How many of us are judgmental about our brothers and sisters at church? And how often do bodies of Christ split because someone could not forgive? How many times does God forgive us? We cannot fulfill the law of love and enjoy our blessings if we have not forgiven ourselves and others around us from our heart. This is a high priority to the soldier coming home. This is vital to holiness and righteousness before God. We cannot understand God or know Him fully unless we have forgiven ourselves and others totally and completely.

The Apostle Paul prayed, "And may you have the power to understand, as all God's people should, how wide, how long, how high, and how deep his love is. May you experience the love of Christ, though it is too great to understand fully. Then you will be made complete with all the fullness of life and power that comes from God." Ephesians 3: 18

This book is for the soldier coming home, his family, and for those in deep depression, rage, or addictions and alcoholism. I would like to say, "Welcome home." God has his arms open wide for you with a tender, loving, kind heart. Whether you are coming home from war or from your dealer's house and you need forgiveness this is a good <u>starting place</u>. It does not matter what you have done or where you have been, the Father's arms are open wide to you. If you are sick and tired of making the same mistakes over and over, then this little book is for you. Are you ready for a supernatural change in your heart and life?

Forgiveness for Our Enemies

In Matthew, Jesus talks about revenge. He says that if a soldier requires you to carry his pack one mile, carry it two miles. He is talking about being good to your enemies.

"If a soldier demands that you carry his gear for a mile, carry it two miles." Matthew 5: 41 Jesus.

Roman occupation was cruel. Rebellious leaders were crucified. But, Jesus said to be good to them. Even though Jesus knew that he would be crucified on the cross and what was ahead at the hands of 400 soldiers; his beating, his whipping, his beard being ripped out, them mocking him, a crown of thorns shoved and pressed into his head, spitting on him, spitting in his face, slapping him in the face with his thorns on his 'crowned' head, hitting him, cursing him, and when the soldiers were finished, Jesus did not even look human. And Jesus never said a word. No one has suffered at the hands of his enemies like Jesus did, and Jesus was wise enough to forgive his enemies and allow God to handle revenge. Jesus asked for his enemies to be forgiven. On the cross, as Jesus was dying he prayed for his enemies.

Jesus said, "Father, forgive them, for they don't know what they are doing." And the soldiers gambled for his clothes by throwing dice. Luke 23: 34

And yet, knowing all this would happen, Jesus said in Matthew, "Carry (his gear) two miles." God took care of Jesus' enemies. The Roman Empire fell.

God's revenge was to destroy and scatter the Jews around the world and grant the Kingdom of God to the whole world. His plan was to bless us with salvation, healing, his glory, the 'Blessing', prosperity, and everything we needed to reach the suffering world by sending His Son to the cross as the last and perfect sacrifice. Then after Jesus' resurrection and glorification, the Holy Spirit our comforter, and great joy, were sent. God's perfect revenge was salvation for the world through Jesus' sacrifice and suffering, first to the Jews then to the whole world.

Saul, who later became the "Apostle Paul", was at the stoning of Stephen, the first martyr, and he was probably in Jerusalem for the Passover and saw the crucifixion of Jesus. Saul looked on the stoning of Stephen, with approval, and then began throwing Christians in jail. Stephen's last prayer was:

... as he fell to his knees, shouting, "Lord, don't charge them with this sin!" And with that he (Stephen) died. Acts 7: 60b

Saul became the Apostle Paul and wrote two-thirds of the New Testament giving his life to the foundation for the gentile church through an eternity of service to the Lord Jesus. Allow God the honor and wisdom of revenge. We must always leave revenge in God's hands.

"I will take revenge; I will pay them back," says the Lord. Instead, "If your enemies are hungry, feed them. If they are thirsty, give them something to drink. In doing this, you will heap burning coals of shame on their heads. Don't let evil conquer you, but conquer evil by doing good." Romans 12:19,20

If we have forgiven our enemies completely we will forget. When we see God's judgment we will feel compassion and not satisfaction. I have seen my enemies suffer: broken bones, paralysis, and even death. We will have a healthy fear of the Lord when we see our enemies suffer. God's judgment is just. What if we are not forgiven or face persecution as we pray for them, or as we go to make restitution or an apology? Rejoice and leave it in God's hands. Pray for your enemies, do good to them that persecute you. Always remember to allow God to judge, turn them over to God in prayer and follow his instructions.

There is also restitution by substitution. If we cannot make restitution in person sometimes we pay it to a third party, for example, a gift to charity or volunteer work. Sometimes God has me do amends, apologies, and restitution to a member of that person's family. Through this we can still learn the lessons God wanted us to learn in the first place. Sometimes a simple apology will do. If we cannot find the person, we pray and God will give us the opportunity. Sometimes we do not have enough money to make restitution. We can make payments or wait and allow God to arrange the restitution. When God opens the door for an apology or restitution, it will be to the right person at the right time. This is God's work, not ours.

Remember, one apology or on restitution at a time under the guidance of a counselor or Pastor, someone wise. Wait until you have finished working all the tools in this book. Apologies and restitutions are last. When you do start making them start with the most simple and easiest until your faith is built to make the more difficult. Forgiveness and love are a life-long journey. <u>This is not something done once and forgotten and neither is it done over-night. There is a lot of work ahead.</u>

Heart to Heart

Alcohol, illegal drugs, sex outside of marriage, violence, rage, anger, and depression complicate forgiveness. It is like trying to put a fire out with gasoline. Sex outside of marriage complicates forgiveness and alcohol and illegal drugs bring down walls of decency. Alcohol and illegal drugs fuel anger, guilt, depression and violence. Anger turned inside is depression, and anger turned outside is rage, and violence. If you have medication for depression, <u>DO NOT STOP TAKING IT WITHOUT MEDICAL SUPERVISION! I am not a doctor.</u> (Sometimes depression is caused by a chemical imbalance in the brain. Forgiveness, and coming off illegal drugs and alcohol can help a great deal but some have to take medication for depression and mental illness. Be very careful. I have to take medication and I am good at forgiveness and have come a long way. My doctors reduced my meds in half, but it was under their guidance and supervision).

To overcome depression, anger, and violence caused by resentments one has to feel the guilt and need for repentance to be able to write and talk about true feelings from the inside out. Alcohol and illegal drugs, rage and violence, and sex outside of marriage fuel, hide, and confuse those feelings that need to be exposed. It is wise for many reasons to stay away from all alcohol, illegal drugs, rage, anger, and immoral sex on a daily basis. <u>One day at a time.</u> It is wise not to use <u>any</u> illegal drugs, alcohol, or put yourself into position for violence, or immoral sex. That includes marijuana. Marijuana is an illegal, mind and mood, altering drug. Stay away from it.

Now you may say, "Impossible!! How can I live up to all that?" Well, you can't. This is where God's grace and mercy come in. With God all things are possible. That is what this little book is about. This is a chance for a new beginning. This is the start of a new life.

If you cannot control your addictions there are programs to help. Alcoholics Anonymous, Narcotics Anonymous, Sex Anonymous, and Teen Challenge are proven by millions to work. I suggest starting there. Sometimes it takes a 'bunch of drunks' to teach us how to stop abusing drugs, alcohol, sex, people, and 'put the plug in the jug' learning how to forgive and forget. I had to sober up and feel my deep feelings, too, to be able to forgive and deal with violence in my home. Forgiveness was most the battle. I first had to forgive myself and then everyone around me, but I had to do it sober and celibate. I could have no crutches, but had to depend on God to truly forgive and become a different person. I had to rely on God. And feelings never killed anyone. I had to face the pain without running and hiding. The person I wanted to be was someone I could look in the mirror and be comfortable with, who I was and how God saw me…..Precious to Him.

If you are not ready, may this book be a good starting place for you……….

This is what the Bible, God's Word, says about sex, drugs, and alcohol. The last part is Proverbs 31, the wife to look for in a spouse. What wives should look like for us Christians. This is what we should strive for.

"Follow my advice, my son; always treasure my commands. Obey my commands and live! Guard my instructions as you guard your own eyes. Tie them on your fingers as a reminder. Write them deep within your heart. Love wisdom like a sister; make insight a beloved member of your family. Let them protect you from an affair with an immoral woman, from listening to the flattery of a promiscuous woman. While I was at the window of my house, looking through the curtain, I saw some naïve young men, and one in particular who lacked common sense. He was crossing the street near the house of an immoral woman, strolling down the path by her house. It was twilight, in the evening, as deep darkness fell. The woman approached him, seductively dressed and sly of heart. She was the brash, rebellious type, never content to stay at home. She is often in the streets and markets, soliciting at every corner. She threw her arms around him and kissed him, and with a brazen look she said, "I've just made my peace offerings and fulfilled my vows. You're the one I was looking for! I came out to find you, and here you are! My bed is spread with beautiful blankets, with colored sheets of Egyptian linen. I've perfumed my bed with myrrh, aloes, and cinnamon. Come, let's drink our fill of love until morning. Let's enjoy each other's caresses, for my husband is not home. He's away on a long trip. He has taken a wallet full of money with him and won't return until later this month. So she seduced him with her pretty speech and enticed him with her flattery. He followed her at once, like an ox going to the slaughter. He was like a stag caught in a trap, awaiting the arrow that would pierce its heart. He was like a bird flying into a snare little knowing it would cost him his life. So listen to me, my sons, and pay attention to my words. Don't let your hearts stray away toward her. Don't wander down her wayward path. For she has been the ruin of many; many men have been her victims. Her house is the road to the grave. Her bedroom is the den of death."

Proverbs 7

"Who has anguish? Who has sorrow? Who is always fighting? Who is always complaining? Who has unnecessary bruises? Who has bloodshot eyes? It is the one who spends long hours in the taverns, trying out new drinks. Don't gaze at the wine, seeing how red it is, how it sparkles in the cup, how smoothly it goes down. For in the end it bites like a poisonous snake, it stings like a viper. You will see hallucinations, and you will say crazy things. You will stagger like a sailor tossed at sea, clinging to a swaying mast. And you will say, 'They hit me, but I didn't feel it. I didn't even know it when they beat me up. When will I wake up so I can look for another drink?'"

Proverbs 23: 29-35

"The sayings of King Lemuel contain this message, which his mother taught him.

O my son, O son of my womb. O son of my vows, do not waste your strength on women, on those who ruin kings. It is not for kings, O Lemuel, to guzzle wine. Rulers should not crave alcohol. For if they drink, they may forget the law and not give justice to the oppressed. Alcohol is for the dying and wine for those in bitter distress. Let them drink to forget their poverty and remember their troubles no more. Speak up for those who cannot speak for themselves; ensure justice for those being crushed. Yes, speak up for the poor and helpless, and see that they get justice.

Who can find a virtuous and capable wife? She is more precious than rubies. Her husband can trust her, and she will greatly enrich his life. She brings him good, not harm all the days of her life. She finds wool and flax and busily spins it. She is like a merchant's ship, bringing her food from afar. She gets up before dawn to prepare breakfast for her household and plan the day's work for her servant girls. She goes to inspect a field and buys it with her earnings she plants a vineyard. She is energetic and strong, a hard worker. She makes sure her dealings are profitable, her lamp burns late into the night. Her hands are busy spinning thread, her fingers twisting fiber. She extends a helping hand to the poor and opens her arms to the needy. She has no fear of winter for her household for everyone has warm cloths. She makes her own bedspreads. She dresses in fine linen and purple gowns. He husband is well known at the city gates, where he sits with the other civic leaders. She makes belted linen garments and sashes to sell to the merchants. She is clothed with strength and dignity, and she laughs without fear of the future. When she speaks, her words are wise and she gives instructions with kindness. She carefully watches everything in her household and suffers nothing from laziness. Her children stand and bless her. Her husband praises her. "There are many virtuous and capable women in the world, but you surpass them all!" Charm is deceptive, and beauty does not last; but a woman who fears the Lord will be greatly praised. Reward her for all she has done. Let her deeds publicly declare her praise.

Proverbs 31

Tools for Forgiveness

It is time to begin writing. I first wrote out my "story of pain." I wrote about all the hurt I had suffered in my life. I wrote everything that haunted me, the people that I blamed, including myself. I wrote about my failures and how others had hurt me. I also wrote about my fears. I put all my fears on paper: past, present, and future fears and worries. I wrote about my mistakes, sins, and painful things I could not forget and did not want to remember. I wrote down; my resentments (relived anger), fears, worries, mistakes and sins that could not be forgiven nor forgotten, things that bothered or haunted me, and the things I did that I could not get off my mind. I did a thorough work on my rage, anger, people, and things I had destroyed. I wrote them all down. Go ahead and pour out your heart and hold nothing back. This should take a few weeks, or a month or two. When I could think of nothing else, I would lay down my pen and wait a few days. Prayer helps a lot. I listened to my heart and waited a while. I knew when I was finished with my story. Keep your work where no one will find it, this is between you and God. Pray as you write and leave nothing out. This is a way God can get into your heart and clean up the mess. Like I said, "This is between you and God."

Depression is anger turned inside. I also wrote the things people did to me or said to me that made me feel unworthy. I wrote about how others had treated me and how I felt about it. I had to "dig" around in my insides and see exactly who and what they said or did that hurt me. Then I had to look at the truth, which made me feel much better. Humility is honesty and truth about something or someone. It was a great relief to me to know I was precious and unique in God's eyes no matter who said I was unworthy. Then, of course, I could forgive them and receive complete healing. A study of who we are in Christ and a revelation of how much God loves us can go a long way in our healing and give us value again.

After I was finished with my story, holding back nothing and being thorough, I then put it in "Chart" form. This gave me organization in my thoughts and I could see patterns. This helped me a great deal in seeing my resentments, and resentments are relived anger. I put them in black and white. These charts also showed me exactly who I was angry with, why, and later, what my part in the bitterness was. After I finished with the charts, I found someone outside my family who was trustworthy and wise. Maybe a Chaplain or Counselor, someone I respected and I knew would not share my life's story with anyone. Someone I admired and wanted to be like someday. Someone much wiser than I, someone I could trust, and I shared my secrets, holding nothing back. If this person does not work out, go find someone else, but get it all out and do not hold back.

TOOL # ONE
RESENTMENT CHART
RELIVED ANGER= HONESTY

A.   Who _____

B.   Why _____

_____

_____

C.   What was my part? _____

_____

_____

D.   What was being threatened? _____

      1.   Money

      2.   Self-Esteem

      3.   Ambition

      4.   Personal Relationships

      5.   Sexual Relationships

      6.   Peace of Mind

      7.   Peace of Soul

      8.   Safety

RESENTMENT CHART
RELIVED ANGER= HONESTY

E. Who _____

F. Why _____

_____

_____

G. What was my part? _____

_____

_____

H. What was being threatened? _____

    9. Money

    10. Self-Esteem

    11. Ambition

    12. Personal Relationships

    13. Sexual Relationships

    14. Peace of Mind

    15. Peace of Soul

    16. Safety

RESENTMENT CHART
RELIVED ANGER= HONESTY

I. Who _____

J. Why _____

_____

_____

K. What was my part? _____

_____

_____

L. What was being threatened? _____

    17. Money

    18. Self-Esteem

    19. Ambition

    20. Personal Relationships

    21. Sexual Relationships

    22. Peace of Mind

    23. Peace of Soul

    24. Safety

Resentment Chart
Relived Anger= Honesty

M.   Who _____

N.   Why _____

_____

_____

O.   What was my part? _____

_____

_____

P.   What was being threatened? _____

      25. Money

      26. Self-Esteem

      27. Ambition

      28. Personal Relationships

      29. Sexual Relationships

      30. Peace of Mind

      31. Peace of Soul

      32. Safety

Resentment Chart
Relived Anger= Honesty

Q.   Who _____

R.   Why _____

_____

_____

S.   What was my part? _____

_____

_____

T.   What was being threatened? _____

        33. Money

        34. Self-Esteem

        35. Ambition

        36. Personal Relationships

        37. Sexual Relationships

        38. Peace of Mind

        39. Peace of Soul

        40. Safety

RESENTMENT CHART
RELIVED ANGER= HONESTY

U.   Who _____

V.   Why _____

_____

_____

W.   What was my part? _____

_____

_____

X.   What was being threatened? _____

     41. Money

     42. Self-Esteem

     43. Ambition

     44. Personal Relationships

     45. Sexual Relationships

     46. Peace of Mind

     47. Peace of Soul

     48. Safety

RESENTMENT CHART
RELIVED ANGER = HONESTY

Y.   Who _____

Z.   Why _____

_____

_____

AA.   What was my part? _____

_____

_____

AB.   What was being threatened? _____

49. Money

50. Self-Esteem

51. Ambition

52. Personal Relationships

53. Sexual Relationships

54. Peace of Mind

55. Peace of Soul

56. Safety

RESENTMENT CHART
RELIVED ANGER= HONESTY

AC.   Who _____

AD.   Why _____

_____

_____

AE.   What was my part? _____

_____

_____

AF.   What was being threatened? _____

      57. Money

      58. Self-Esteem

      59. Ambition

      60. Personal Relationships

      61. Sexual Relationships

      62. Peace of Mind

      63. Peace of Soul

      64. Safety

Fears

"Resist the devil and he will flee from you."

1. _____

_____

2. _____

_____

3. _____

_____

4. _____

_____

5. _____

_____

6. _____

_____

7. _____

_____

8. _____

_____

9. _____

_____

10. _____

_____

11._____

_____

12._____

_____

13._____

_____

14._____

_____

Mistakes or sins that I cannot forgive or forget
Mercy

1. Against myself because _____

    _____

2. Against my spouse because _____

    _____

3. Against my children because_____

    _____

4. Against my x-spouse because _____

    _____

5. Against my parents because _____

    _____

6. Against these family members because _____

    _____

7. Against my friends because _____

    _____

8. Against these institutions because _____

    _____

9. Against these others because _____

    _____

10. Against my employer and co-workers because_____

_____

11. Against God because _____

_____

People, Circumstances, or Things
That Bother me or Haunt me
And Why
"If we confess our sins, He is faithful and just to forgive us."

1. _____

_____

_____

_____

2. _____

_____

_____

_____

3. _____

_____

_____

_____

4. _____

_____

_____

_____

5. _____

_____

_____

_____

6. _____

_____

_____

_____

7. _____

_____

_____

_____

8. _____

_____

_____

_____

People, Worries, or Situations I Cannot Change, Control, or Get off my mind
"Be of good cheer for I have overcome the world," Jesus.

1. a. Who _____

    b. What _____

    c. Why _____

    _____

    _____

2. a. Who _____

    b. What _____

    c. Why _____

    _____

    _____

3. a. Who _____

    b. What _____

    c. Why _____

    _____

    _____

4. a. Who _____

    b. What _____

    c. Why _____

    _____

    _____

5. a. Who _____

    b. What _____

    c. Why _____

    _____

    _____

Tool # Two

A.   Mercy-

Have compassion and see the other person's side of the situation. God has had mercy on you. Maybe the other person is suffering, or in great fear.

"Father God, please forgive me for being so selfish and self-centered that I did not see the other person's side of the story and have mercy on them as you have had mercy on me. Show me how to grow in compassion for other people. In Jesus' precious name and blood. Amen."

B.   Holiness-

What was my part? What was my mistake and sin? This is where a Pastor or Chaplain or Counselor can help you with your blind spots with each situation one at a time, and bring character defects out in the open as you grow spiritually towards a clear conscience. Holiness.

1. Pride

2. Anger

3. Greed

4. Resentment

5. Gluttony

6. Shame

7. Fear

8. Lust

9. Self-pity

10. Selfishness

11. Self-Centeredness

12. Envy

13. Jealousy

14. Laziness

15. Religious

16. Hypocrisy

Tool # Three

Prayer–

"God, please forgive me for my sins, character defects, and trespasses as I forgive those who have trespassed against me. Bring good out of all this hurt and anger. Bring good out of this mess, as you forgive me, heal me, and heal all my relationships. In Jesus' name. Amen".

A.   Now ask yourself:

  1. What did I say or do to other people that I need to apologize for?

  2. What kind of restitution do I need to make?

> A. Living Amends?
>
> B. Apology?
>
> C. Financial Restitution?
>
> D. All three?

C. Fill out the following charts and then, under the supervision of a Pastor, Chaplain, or Counselor, begin making your apologies and restitution <u>one at a time</u>. Make all apologies and restitution face-to-face if at all possible. And if someone does not accept your apology or throws you out, that is okay. These tools are for you to grow in peace and God will honor you. The first should be the easiest and as your faith grows, and as you enjoy a clear conscience, tackle the more difficult ones as you go. If you cannot find the people you need to see, pray and wait. God is the healer and will arrange miracles for you to find and make your apologies to each and every one. If you owe money and do not have enough to pay for all the restitution, again, make the small ones first and as your faith grows, God is the healer and will arrange a way. If you have the money to make restitution but it looks impossible to make the apology, for example: if that person has died, or you cannot find them, or they live far away, or it was a childhood sin like stealing when you were young, or it is to a store that has gone out of business, or an institution or a group of people, then make the restitution to a third party. For example: If they died by cancer, make a donation to an institution for cancer research, you can also visit the grave and make apologies and give the money to a living relative, or if it was against a child and you cannot find that person or they refuse to see you, make a gift to a ministry or those who do volunteer work with children. You may need to volunteer with an organization, for some time maybe, instead of giving money. Volunteer work softens the heart and allows compassion to grow for those less fortunate than you. And it is fun! God will show you how to make amends and grow spiritually when things look impossible. And this is great for the spiritual; faith, love, compassion, peace, and forgiveness to grow in your heart as you make peace with God and your fellow man. You will have great peace. Your life will change 100%, I guarantee.

CAUTION!!!!!!!! USE THESE TOOLS IN ORDER!!!!!DO NOT START TOOL #2 UNTIL YOU HAVE THOROUGHLY COMPLETED TOOL #1!!!!!AND DO NOT START TOOL #3 UNTIL YOU HAVE THOROUGHLY COMPLETED TOOL #2!!!! DO THEM IN ORDER!!! AND WHEN YOU ARE SATISFIED WITH TOOL #3, THAT YOU HAVE DONE AS MUCH AS POSSIBLE IN YOUR APOLOGIES AND RESTITUTIONS, GO BACK TO TOOL #1. SEE IF THE LORD BRINGS ANYTHING TO MIND THAT YOU NEED TO WORK ON (IF YOUR CONSCIENCE BOTHERS YOU, OR THERE IS MORE TO DO, OR IF THERE ARE ANY NEW RESENTMENTS OR ANGER--AND THERE WILL BE!!!) GO BACK TO TOOL #1 AND BEGIN WORKING ON THE NEW RESENTMENTS AND ANGER. THIS IS A LIFE-TIME PROCESS OF LOVE AND FORGIVENESS. YOU DO NOT NEED TO DO IT PERFECTLY AND THEN STOP BUT THROUGHOUT LIFE YOU WILL NEED THESE TOOLS OVER AND OVER AGAIN. I PROMISE. NO ONE IS PERFECT, AND WE ALL GET MAD OR OFFENDED ALMOST EVERY DAY, EVEN THE BEST OF US, AND THE MOST RIGHTEOUS AND HOLY HAVE SIN IN THEIR LIVES, TOO, SO WE STRIVE FOR PROGRESS EACH DAY, AND PEACE AND THE PRESENCE OF GOD GETS MORE INTENSE AS WE USE THESE TOOLS. THERE IS GREAT REWARD AHEAD OF YOU.

Repentance

1. To whom do I owe an apology? _____

2. What did I do? _____

   _____

   _____

3. What kind of restitution do I need to make? _____

   a. Living amends where I stop the behavior?

   b. Apology?

   c. Financial restitution?

4. To whom do I owe an apology? _____

5. What did I do? _____

   _____

   _____

6. What kind of restitution do I need to make? _____

   d. Living amends where I stop the behavior?

   e. Apology?

   f. Financial restitution?

7. To whom do I owe an apology? _____

8. What did I do? _____

   _____

   _____

9. What kind of restitution do I need to make? _____

   g. Living amends where I stop the behavior?

   h. Apology?

   i. Financial restitution?

10. To whom do I owe an apology? _____

11. What did I do? _____

   _____

   _____

12. What kind of restitution do I need to make? _____

   j. Living amends where I stop the behavior?

   k. Apology?

   l. Financial restitution?

13. To whom do I owe an apology? _____

14. What did I do? _____

   _____

   _____

15. What kind of restitution do I need to make? _____

   m. Living amends where I stop the behavior?

   n. Apology?

   o. Financial restitution?

16. To whom do I owe an apology? _____

17. What did I do? _____

_____

_____

18. What kind of restitution do I need to make? _____

   p.   Living amends where I stop the behavior?

   q.   Apology?

   r.   Financial restitution?

19. To whom do I owe an apology? _____

20. What did I do? _____

_____

_____

21. What kind of restitution do I need to make? _____

   s.   Living amends where I stop the behavior?

   t.   Apology?

   u.   Financial restitution?

22. To whom do I owe an apology? _____

23. What did I do? _____

_____

_____

24. What kind of restitution do I need to make? _____

   v.   Living amends where I stop the behavior?

   w.   Apology?

   x.   Financial restitution?

How Many Times?

"If another believer sins, rebuke that person then if there is repentance, forgive. Even if that person wrongs you seven times a day and each time turns again and asks, you MUST forgive," Jesus said.

Luke 17:3, 4

Then Peter came to him and asked, "Lord, how often should I forgive someone who sins against me? Seven times?"

"No not seven times," Jesus replied, "but seventy times seven!"

Matthew 18: 21, 22

In other words, forget it and walk in forgiveness!!!! When you finish the work outlined briefly in this book, do not stop there. Each day you will come into hurt, fear, and pain. Keep this little instruction booklet and make it a daily practice until you are quick to forgive and it is your nature to forgive. Then you can begin to experience the compassion Jesus has in his heart for you and your fellow man. You will experience his great wealth of healing and peace in your spirit, soul, and body. You will see the cross differently and you will be different, a peculiar people full of grace and compassion. As you grow in character Jesus will become more real to you and your faith will grow.

Keep this little book and use it as a little instructional book on forgiveness, compassion, and character development.

70 x 7

A Message for the Family

I have four Veterans in my immediate family. I have dealt with many different situations and have found some success. I would like to tackle three major concerns. One is the need for smooth entry back into life from deployment and time in the military, two is violent behavior in the home, and the last, when our loved ones shut us out. I will share with you some of the things I did that were successful and some things that I believe only the military can solve.

First of all, I would like to discuss smooth entry into life after deployment and military service. I would like to say that the answers I found were in the Bible and seeing the success that our WWII Veterans had. One of the reasons that the WWII Veterans were able to avoid a lot of problems we see today was because they were brought home in boats and in groups. These men were together for a long time and were able to talk things out with each other before they came home. They got some rest and recreation after they put down their weapons and were able to spend some time talking things out with each other. Our soldiers coming home now lay down their weapons and are back into society within hours. Many are alone. We especially saw this happen in our Vietnam Vets and thought that the reaction of society was the reason for their problems that our WWII Vets did not have. That is incorrect. Our Vietnam Vets were home on the streets within hours after laying down their weapons and alone to survive any way they could. Today our Veterans are coming home and facing a good homecoming, yes, but they too, are home within hours after putting down the weapons and facing culture shock. The military needs to prepare our men and women for coming home with the same care they took in training them for their first deployment. Sometimes it is more frightening to come home than to face the enemy because they train for months and even years before the first fight, yet, when coming home there is no preparation for the culture shock and responsibilities facing them.

Think of it this way. For years you are in the military and are surrounded with "fathers", "brothers", and "sisters" who are facing the same things you are. You always have the loyalty of others and someone is there to "watch your back." You are in life and death stress and trauma for years and always have a weapon. Then one day, all of a sudden, you lay down your weapon and in a few hours you are in an airport at home surrounded by civilians and now, how do you survive the shock? You come home and there are no more enemies. No more training to fight. No one fixes your meals. And for the first time since being 18 or 19, you have to think of things like rent, car payment, a job, electricity, food, and if you have a family….. It is a totally different world. And you are surrounded by people who do not understand nor can relate, except maybe the V.A. and they have no answers. Our Veterans need some help from the military itself. Our President needs letters from concerned citizens that the military gets as much care before their separation as they had before their first fight. Families cannot give the type of care and understanding and help in adjusting they need. The government is "dumping" its military into society and trying to make up for it with hospitals, doctors, nurses, social workers, and therapists who cannot relate and are overworked. Our Veterans need healing that only a little time and each other can give. I believe in the long run we would be saving, not only lives and families, but also money, which is the "bottom-line" for the government. Bring our soldiers home in boats and make some 'safe havens' for them and give them time to relax and get used to not carrying a weapon or looking over their shoulder for the enemy. Give them some time and guidance to make goals and mentally get ready for the culture shock they will soon face. Prepare them for their release from trauma and stress.

As a family member, I would suggest placing yourself in your loved one's shoes and not "push" but understand and listen. I would also get involved in writing letters to Congressmen and leaders who could change policies and give our Vets what they need, not only in war, but also in coming home. I have seen the same reaction in Vets who did not go to war, but in peace time. They have problems that affect their whole lives, this is not just a problem in war, but also in peace time, too. We need to care for all our Vets whether coming home from war or peace-time service. This problem will not be solved for years and I do not believe anyone can have more influence and care as the family members of the military.

I have seen some healing in being able to talk to someone. Without judgment, a listening ear can do miracles. And do not turn your loved one over to a doctor, medicine and therapy, and think that will solve the problem. A Vet needs all the listening and understanding and trust he or she can find. Sit down and get your Vet to talk about what they experienced. Without saying more than, "Tell me about…" your Vet may open up and heal where no therapist or doctor can reach in years of medicine and therapy. Above all do not preach. Allow your prayers and witness of a Christ-like life be the power they need to recover. They need trust and hope.

Now, about violence. All four veterans in my immediate family have been violent at one time or another in their lives. I have found my answers in the Bible. Before Jesus was two years old,

King Herod was trying to kill him. All Jesus' life people were plotting to have him destroyed and yet no one could touch him until he laid down his life voluntarily for the sins of the world. <u>I needed to know that kind of protection and love for my veterans</u>. First of all, Joseph and Mary did run. When King Herod was planning to destroy all the children two and under in Bethlehem, Joseph and Mary took Jesus to Egypt and stayed there until King Herod died. So there is a time to leave and a time to stay. With one of my veterans being violent, he was abusive mentally and emotionally while having affairs and not even trying to hide them. I finally left and went to a shelter. I was educated on what abuse was and what value I had by the Salvation Army. After I had been gone for a few months my Vet decided to change and I went home. Another time a Vet in my family was abusive, it was physically. I put a restraining order on him for six months and it was the best thing I could have done. But this Vet did not change. A few years later I began having problems with him again. So I prayed for him and treated him the way Jesus taught us to treat our enemies. I avoided him as much as possible until I could forgive him with all my heart. It was my responsibility to pray for him, do good deeds for him, and forgive him. I know that when I forgive someone with all my heart I will also forget and heal, too. It is God's job to judge and not mine. It is God's job to avenge and not mine. There are times to stay and pray and there are times to leave for a season. Then there are times to leave for good for self-preservation, especially if there are children involved. Only prayer and wisdom can call the shots. I do not believe someone has the right to yell, scream, hit, or threaten me or my children for any reason. We do not deserve it. But I have to look at my own actions and words and see if I am contributing to it. <u>It would be good, and it is my strong suggestion, for each family member to work the tools in this book just as much as a Veteran would for change and forgiveness in their life.</u> Forgiveness is a powerful weapon. Forgiveness is more powerful than a gun or knife. Allowing God to avenge is stronger than any damage I could do. God is just and gives everyone a chance to change before judgment. When someone turns to Him, they are forgiven and changed for the better in their heart which is wiser and more beneficial than anything I could do. That is why prayer and forgiveness is so powerful. God's love is Supreme. My Vet did not change. He is now institutionalized. I do not live in fear any more.

Two of my military family members have shut me out. One came home and the other has not, yet. The Vet who came home had moved to another city and told all his friends that his family was dead. We did not hear from him for years and it broke my Mother's heart. I found a scripture in Proverbs that says "… to give an angry man a gift and a bribe under the table pacifies the strongest fury." So, I sent a letter once a month and then a present once a year. I just kept the letters positive about home and did not ask him to come home or what he was doing. I was doing it all in faith. Then I got involved in some work with other Veterans and accidently met some of my Veteran's friends (or I should say, "God dropped me down into the middle of some of his closest friends"). I did not ask any questions about how he was doing or where he was, I just gave my attention to his friends, as I would anyone else, and cared for them as best I knew how. Then one day, unexpectedly, my Veteran came home. He was addicted to alcohol, drugs, divorced eight times, could not hold a job, and was violent. <u>I believe God has to get us ready for our loved one's return as well as prepare them for coming home.</u> I never pushed or suffocated. It was his decision to come home. I believe God was strengthening me, <u>more than him,</u> for his homecoming.

"70 x 7"

Jesus.